A Presentment of Englishry

Liam Guilar

A Presentment of Englishry

Shearsman Books

First published in the United Kingdom in 2019 by
Shearsman Books
50 Westons Hill Drive
Emersons Green
BRISTOL
BS16 7DF

Shearsman Books Ltd Registered Office
30–31 St. James Place, Mangotsfield, Bristol BS16 9JB
(this address not for correspondence)

www.shearsman.com

ISBN 978-1-84861-662-2

Copyright © Liam Guilar, 2019.

The right of Liam Guilar to be identified as the author
of this work has been asserted by him in accordance with the
Copyrights, Designs and Patents Act of 1988.
All rights reserved.

Contents

The Red Queen — 7

Interlude Number One:
Three Stories from Gerald of Wales — 23

An Preost Wes On Leodan — 27

Fathers — 43

Interlude Number Two:
Two Stories From Bede — 83

Fragments — 87

Coda: Presentment of Englishry — 107

Notes — 109

The Red Queen

(*The Bronze Age*)

1.

Where the morning light slabs off the water
a broken, blinding dazzle,
along the wharves the empty wooden ships
tug at their moorings on the tide,
like sleepy dogs testing their chains.
The sunlight coming off the bay
burns the eyes until at noon
a man finds shelter in a tavern
where the wine is sour, the bread stale
but the storytellers talk of Ictus:
hard travelling for the best of tin.
One trip will set you up for life
if the captain and his crew are bold.
'And you survive.'

Albion, island of fog and rain,
where the painted people worship their red queen.
'She eats men at the equinox.'
'Earth Mother', 'Earth Goddess',
'Nightmare bitch in barely human form.'
They pause and pass the wine.
'Torchlight, under the trees,
in her sacred grove by the stones of sacrifice
with the heads of her enemies keeping their blind watch,
impaled on the rings of blood-caked poles.'

Few have made the journey.
Sunbaked salted men, patient and watchful,
should one be present: nods, smiles, saying nothing.
Why spoil a story that keeps the fools at home?

Comes a merchant with some goods to barter
buying drinks in search of information

eager for hard travelling.
Addicted to the long journey,
the prize a flicker on the border
where the daylight world
blurs into myth and nightmare.

Panning for gold amongst the dross
knowing a well-told lie's as plausible
as the hesitant truth,
and often more believable.

'There are two ways to reach Ictus,'
says the local expert, 'both are long and hard.'
'And both are dangerous,' adds another.
Sail west through the Pillars of Hercules
into the raging swirl of Ocean.
Head north, keeping the coast in sight
until you see white cliffs to the west.
Run hard for them,
turn south and west again, along the fractured coast.

'Or, head inland; load your cargo onto mules,
hire muscle against sudden ambush.
From village to village, where you will be welcomed,
follow the rivers over the watershed
until you reach the sea, then find a ship
with a strong crew and a skilled captain.

Either way you sniff along the coast,
until you see the beacon lights,
lit when the season's right'.

Calculate profit against cost and risk.
What tips the balanced scale?
To measure everything
learnt and known, against the unpredictable

and succeed: the pleasures of its doing
salted by fear?

Courage without calculation is rank stupidity,
risk without awareness is a fool
blundering blindfold on a cliff edge.

The men whose ships
rot with their corpses on the seabed,
calculated risk, skill against circumstance.
Those who lose have nothing to regret.
Better to go down on the long voyage out
than grow old at home.

2

He followed the trade route inland,
pack mules and armed guards
the excitement of beginning
blurring into trudgery.
Over the watershed, risking the winter crossing.
It was so cold that language froze.
High on the pass, around their campfires
lips moved but no words cracked that silence.
Slaves perished. Some turned back.
But sure-footed guides, their confidence a mystery,
stepped into fog on the nebulous path.
Their animals fearful, reluctant
but leading down, out of the clouds,
into the wooded valley.
The river still frozen. Ice on the rocks.
They shook with the fierce elation
of surviving terror.

The wary hospitality of strangers
in wooden shacks where hidden children
watch the traveller's every move.
Nights without sleep. Fear of robbery
in random meetings on the road
where journeys intersect, snippets of a story
that move on.
Huddled around inadequate fires at night
remembering sunlight, but holding to the line
drawn on the rough wooden table
by a grubby finger.

To reach the unfamiliar coast,
where the light comes off grey water.
Here the wind carries the smell of recent rain

and the fading taste of winter.
Wood smoke stings the nostrils
cutting the dull stench of wool that never dries.
Here men huddle along the wharves
shivering for the sailing season.
For the storms to cease,
for the wind to die and turn.
Their myths are of the amber to the north
and the spice trail to the east.
The crossing to Albion their commonplace.
(A few have made the longer haul to Ictus).

How to choose a captain and a crew?
Athena does not guide his steps
nudge his elbow or whisper in his ear.

How to tell a brave man from the reckless fool?
The expert from the actor? Easy in a crisis,
but that's a bad time to learn that you were wrong.

Again the merchant patiently sifts the stories.
Clatter of laughter, stale smell of wine,
the women for hire move around the tables
hover, moving on. Indifferent to their call,
hooked on the erotics of profit and risk
the subtle rhythms of movement over distance.
And once again there comes the time to roll the dice.

This captain was no different to the others.
He had been to the Amber coast
and was ready to try the dash to Ictus.
Intrigued by the challenge,
willing to step off the edge of the world
to see what lies over the lip.
Deal done. The sailing explained,
the course outlined in detail
'You will see two fires.

One on Ictus, one on the mainland.
At low tide a man can walk between them
If he knows the route and hurries.
Step wrongly, loiter and he dies.'

The rules of trade remembered and rehearsed
but then a softer voice, 'There are strange things
that happen there. Strange, gentle things,
you will remember and yet not believe.'

'Swift black ships on a wine dark sea',
My calloused arse, my cracked and bleeding hands.
Whoever sang that line never foundered
on the wrong side of a headland
with the wind onshore, a sludging swell
the colour of a hangover trying to retch them up
onto the rocks. All hands to fend her off, and pray
to whatever God was listening
to shift the wind around before her timbers stove.
Or moved, sun starved and shivering,
when holding a course was wishful thinking
through the ash-grey fog, each oar dip amplified
by the dense and sodden silence they were clawing through.

3

The painted people had been waiting:
a vibrant hedge along the cliff top.
Drums, horns, cries of welcome,
to show them kindness helped them drag their ship
up on the shelving beach and set up camp
out of the wind, clear unobstructed views
the grey sea, forever driven to the land
which sends it back, unwanted,
a halo of birds above the headland
the dark green roll away beyond
towards forest as a dark strip on the skyline.

In the shelter of the stones, on the gravelled space
smoothed by centuries of trade
they spread their wares.
Tin, and food, and the trade was good.
Both sides trusting to the courtesies:
mutual pleasure, mutual profit:
fair exchange, no robbery.
With death sitting, to one side,
armed and patient,
should the visitors betray their welcome.

On the night after they were done,
the islanders appeared around their campfires.
Fantasy made flesh, stepping from the shadow world.
There was fresh food, strange drink,
music and women, eager for sex.

But the Red Queen bade the Captain follow.
Knowing his death was present he left the music,
laughter, the naked bodies
moving on the firelight's edge

the singing drunks.
Stepped into darkness.

Torches along the causeway. Water
lapping close, cutting against distant surf,
across the arrhythmic splash of their wading.
The headland with its beacon fire rising
upward shelving beach hard sand to soft,
and the steep path to the cliff top.
The wind shook fire and moonlight.
Passing through the ghost fence:
the dead face forward
dedicated to their watch.
Here, said the Queen, the sea will meet the land.
A group waited in silence:
two upright stones, one capping them,
framing the darker slit of an entrance.

She handed him a beaker full of wine.

A door of ivory is moved aside.
He stalled, confronting darkness.

Go in. Be welcomed.
We promise you no harm.
Refuse our gift,
insult our Goddess
and you die here.
The spears for emphasis.

Better to meet death going forward,
better to die knowing than stranded
on the outside of a mystery.
Stooping, he squeezed himself
between the fringe of grass and moss
smoothed stone against his fingertips,
roof closing in, the drag on his calves

telling him the floor was sloping down
unsteady as the light behind him failed.
He reached a narrowing and saw a dimmer light ahead.
Twisting he forced himself between the rocks
slippery with moss, the water dripping from above,
knew he emerged into space. Dizzy,
high above, a small hole admitted moonlight
the dim curve of the roof, falling circular space,
and the figure waiting at its centre,
moonlit shadow and warm flesh,
a female sitting on a bed of furs.
Between them a small brazier
picked out the mask she wore.
A hood, with slits for eyes, nose, mouth.
Her long hair, braided, falling down one shoulder
to her naked breast.

Welcome.
Rippling round the cave, delayed echo.
Small hands scatter leaves onto the coals.
Frail strands of smoke struggled to climb the light
and failed to reach the stars. A sudden taste of iron.
Lust slipping from the shadows, clawing at his throat
bent him double. On the edge of the whirlpool
he gave way to the drag that pulled him down
dissolved him as he flowed towards her.
Welcome, welcome, you are welcome.
She rocked towards him as though pulling at a tether.
Her words shimmering on the catch of her own breath.

An awkward blur of mouths, hands,
his, hers, hard to tell, delirium
moonlight flesh and shadows
turned to water. She smelt of fresh rain,
grave earth, spring flood.
Sinuous, turbulent, strong.
He held a river in his arms

carrying him as flotsam on its heaving surface
until the ragged sound of his own breathing
like a ship's timbers rubbing against a wharf
broke the steady sound of the nearby sea.

He will remember this night,
the way you'd remember a dream
twelve months after you woke from it,
but nothing
(except his own death),
would ever be so real.

                        At night, a man fleeing
from hounds and the hatred of his enemies,
through tangled undergrowth,
wading through streams, mired,
strength gone, breath lost, legs burning, shaking,
stands sobbing on the wrong side of a door
knows rest and safety are inches more than he can go
but cannot wake the watchman who will let him in.
He batters at the door. Is still battering when the dogs
drag him down and tear his flesh to gobbets.

Frantically trying to reach that place where desire
might be erased. Where indifference
might be possible.
Masked face turned away
the long curve of her throat, small sounds
pleasure-torn, like dark birds startled into flight
rising at dusk over bright water.

4

The morning familiar as cold stone.
Rain drifting through the smoke hole in the roof.
The chamber, damp and hard and stale.
His body ached. Pain behind his eyes,
a strange taste in his mouth. The wine?

He scrabbled towards daylight, wondering
if he'd died. But surely no cold rain fell in heaven.
Outside, one man, leaning on his spear
watching. Rain drops, beading on his nose
dripped from the hand that clutched the shaft.
Three women waited: Mother, Maid and Crone,
patient as the stones they sat on.

He saw his own death flickering on the edges of the light
but mother maid and crone
gently lead him to a hut he hadn't seen.
Inside the same sour smell of something on the brazier
warm water for his bath, oil for his skin
they washed and braided his long hair

This is how you prepare a corpse for burial.

Last night her hands, now theirs, the skilled indifference
wondering if one of them was she without the mask.
If the rhythmic sound he heard was his death being honed.

They sang as they worked, call and answer.
He understood nothing.

Gold anklets and a necklace made of gold
studded with amber. Gold torcs for his arms,

rings, bracelets. All this without a word to him.
This is how you prepare a corpse for burial.

The old one pointed.
When he saw the sack was full of tin
he took it and went on his way.

At low tide, in daylight, the causeway was no mystery.
The journey back much quicker than the journey out.
The bodies of his crew lay scattered round their camp.
No sign of any islanders, no sign they had been here the night before.

He bent and touched the merchant,
who groaned, clutching at his head.
They had no proof their wondrous night was not a dream.
He had no proof, except the sack of tin.
When they awoke, baffled, enchanted, bedazzled
he shared the contents of the bag, not surprised
there was one knuckle for each man. No more no less.

A wind to take them home was blowing steadily.
The light was gentle on the water, soft as her hands
where light and water meet, and something new is made
that still remains unnamed.

The Queen said: 'You may not come this way again.
We've made you rich enough to spend your life in comfort.
No need to risk the sea God's wrath or gamble on the wind.'
'I will return', he said, knowing he could not.

'It will never be the place you left:
the purest water can only be polluted.
A place of dreams that validates the risks you took
and measured what you are?
Once found, this is the place that you must leave.
The memory that will measure every other day
cannot itself be measured.

You'll sail for amber next time, if you sail at all.
Go with our Lady's blessing and our thanks.'
'And if I tried to stay?'

'We have already dressed your corpse.'

If after every storm, such shelter
men would sail in search of cyclones.

Interlude number one:
Three stories from Gerald of Wales

1)

He stepped out into unobstructed wind,
shut and barred the door, half-dragged,
half-carried the defeated child towards
the parapet. His fumbling hand felt stone

felt for the edge and end of stone, found space.
Footsteps on the stair, pounding at the door.
A small crowd in the courtyard, pointing
to a blind man and a child on the castle's

highest tower. The castellan was pleading:
'Give me back my son!' and demanding
to know how the prisoner had escaped.
Blinded and castrated, for a reason

no one could remember, he'd been there so long
he'd been allowed to grope his way around.
No one thought he could be dangerous.
'Give me back my son, my only son, my heir,

and I will set you free.' 'Castrate yourself,'
the blind man raged. 'Castrate yourself or
I will toss your son, your only son, onto the stones below.'
The gathered people saw the blade descend and groaned.

'You've done it?' called the man. 'I have.'
'Where does it hurt?' 'In my groin.' 'You lied.'
The blind man moved the child closer
to the edge. 'Wait,' screamed the lord, 'this time.'

The people saw the blade and groaned again.
'Where does it hurt?' 'In my heart.'
the blind man held the squirming child over space.
'Wait!' The blade descended: the lord bellowed.

'Where does it hurt?' the blind man called.
'In my teeth,' the gasping Castellan replied.
'Now you will never have another child.'
They thought the boy screamed 'father' as he fell.

The blind man leapt into the wind.
Two bodies scattered on the stones.
A monastery now marks the spot
It's called 'The Scene of Sorrows'.

2)

On the night of the storm the hunter took refuge
with his horse and his dogs in the church of Llanafan.
A foolish and irreverent thing, writes Gerald.
(Welsh and Irish saints are so much more
vindictive than the French and English version.)

By morning the affronted saint,
had driven the dogs mad.
and made the huntsman blind.

Although he did penance and prayed for forgiveness
his sight did not return. (*cf* 'vindictive saints' above).
Hoping for a miracle, his friends helped him to Jerusalem,
a red cross sewn into his tunic. Armed and mounted,
they pointed him towards the heathen's battle lines.
He charged, was cut down and died with honour.

3)

On the first night he dreamt.
He put his hand in the hole
beneath the gushing spring
and pulled out a gold torque.

Three nights; the same dream.
After the third, he arose
walked the mile to the spring
and put his hand in the hole.

A snake bit him and he died.
Dreams are like rumours, writes Gerald,
you need to use your common sense.

AN PREOST WES ON LEODAN

(Arely Regis, Worcestershire, 1218 AD)

A Prologue

A dead crow flapping darkly on a wire.
Move closer. An preost in the rain.
Laȝamon by name.
The Severn, bank-full, slurrying past,
hurrying debris down to Worcester.
To his left, Burntthorn brook
leaking through the alders.
Soon Redstone ford will be impossible
even for the ferryman.
He watches the surface bubble and fold,
aware of his coarse woollen robes,
their insistent itch and stink,
aware that everything is moving,
except him.

The boy who holds his horse;
tired, cold, miserable, whines
an intermittent counterpoint.

1

Hit com him on mode; & on his mern ponke
'And it came into his mind.'
Not my mind, not my thought.

I was playing with the big boys.
The next best thing. The one to watch.
Good to have around the court
while the court moved round the country,
and I moved easily between languages.
At home in four: sing us a song, tell us a story.
At home in the cart ruts of a lord's ambition.

The swirl of abrasive egos
calculations whispering in corridors.
The thrill of being one step from success
and another from oblivion.

2

To Ireland, with John, not then a King,
as a clerk in the household of Gerald of Wales;
That lover of bad puns and sordid facts;
'Write it down, boy, write it down.'
Frustration cruelling his humour even then.
'What price intelligence on the open market?
Behold, Christendom's most scintillating intellect
lacking a bishopric, tutoring the Lackland.
who is a very different kind of prick.'

We were there when the Irish Lords came in,
like creatures from the dark edge of a fairy tale
whose heroes danced on the spear points of their enemies
howling defiance at the overwhelming host.
Experts in the night raid and torched thatch
who cared nothing for title deeds
who counted their wealth in well-fed cattle
whose country rolled like the melt of their syntax
'And is as unknowable as that barbarous tongue.'
Expert thieves of other men's wives.
'Write it down, boy, write it down.'
Despised by Gerald: 'Loose-living fornicators,
Christians who don't know Christ or his church.'
Afraid of nothing except the blistering tongue of their poets.
Baffled by the brutality of castle walls
unarmoured, no match for a knight in an open field
but God help that grey rider
if he chased his bare arse into the mist
into his bogs and forests and hilly places
then his armour would become a rusting shell
for the breeding of maggots;
his head a guest at his enemy's feast.

And John, who didn't need to shave, laughed
and pulled their beards and mocked at them.
Killers who didn't need to purchase Flemish muscle
who would have stabbed him where he sat
then fed him to his dogs. He laughed at them.

The Irish Lords, insulted, faded into mist,
perfecting their resentment.

                      The Anglo-Normans
retired to their castles to practise disappointment
because, God knows, in later years they'd live with it.
John and his lackeys getting hammered
safe behind walls. Gerald making puns:
Taxes raised to pay for Knights, wasted on nights.
Money raised for arms, used to raise skirts.
'Not my best, boy, but write it down.'

First Lackland, soon Softsword
then names no Christian would inscribe,
betraying his father, then his brother.
Offending allies by stealing their bride
then losing the largest empire in Christendom.
You taught him well Gerald.
Write that down.

Gerald stayed in Ireland but sent me home.
The court was changed, had started rotting
like those armoured corpses, oak tangled,
in damp Irish woods. Perhaps

I'd laughed at the wrong joke.
Offended the ignorant with knowledge,
perhaps I'd confused someone's daughter
with a palace prostitute.

Blue eyed wonder boy,
fluent in four languages:
no one was listening to a word I said.

Men turned so their lips were hidden
smiles fleeting as cloud shadow moving over corn field
words emptied of meaning, like those barrels of coins
sent to finance John's expedition
wasted on whoremasters and vintners
misspent, misused, gone; noise on the breeze.
Someone was offended. Something Gerald said?
He was beyond their reach and I was not.

He wrote, quoting, or misquoting, Pliny;
'Be thankful boy, the church does not care who your father was.
Talent always rises to the top. [He proved that was a lie.]
Go be a priest, take Wace's book. Improve your French.

Leave noise, and foolish toils There's nothing you can gain at court.
Give yourself to study, boy: if leisure time is sweet
Then study is a sweeter thing than any other business.'

But God's bright shining son could preach
at *Ernleʒe; at æðelen are chirechen*,
and nobody would know.

3

So here I am *on-fest radestone*
at æðelen are chirechen
Noble my arse. It's a tiny red cell
a half day's walk from Worcester.
The manor miles away.
The noble knight is rarely home.

Why here?
The question echoes in the church
repeats itself in wind, in river,
in the way the grass bends and the bushes sway.
Why anywhere?
A tiny stone shell cast up on the river bank
full of damp silence and the stench of candle wax.
Why this task?
Make it into English, improve your French.
The questions rattle off the walls and fade unanswered.
'I will send for you. When the time is right. When it's safe.'
When I have nothing else to do.
I knew Wace gave his book to *Ælienor*
þe wes Henries queen when she was growing old.
Henry was lusting after Rosamonde.
It meant nothing then, just moves in the game
find a patron, hitch your wagon to a name?
Don't ask what happens when the patron falls?
Lean into the wind. Be alive, here now,
by the flooding river.

I have seen able, loyal men devote their lives to a lord
and at day's end, seen them discarded. Not for policy
or purpose, but as thoughtless reflex.
Wace labouring at his history, 14 years of work!
To be told, abruptly, someone else will finish it.

'Once the King treated me well, gave me much, promised more.
If he had given half of what he promised, I would not be poor.'[1]
And I have seen women beautiful, graceful,
keep faith with their lord until they too are thrown away.
What chance do I have?

I lack a Freond; old word for friend and lover.
No gebedda either–no one to wake beside, no one to care for.
I want. Company, conversation, context.
My Lord's servants are no substitute, although
their stories are the magnificence of God's creation.

All is flowing away; an endless gaining and losing.
I want the rock in the river,
Not the tree uprooted by the flood,
rolled downstream, battered, stranded
when the flood subsides.
Perhaps picked up and carried on again.
Perhaps thrown up and left to rot.

Is writing the rock that time will flow around?
Brutus heard the gulls creaking like a broken axle
while his men dragged their ships out of the water.
Hengist knew they promised landfall.
Uther scattered them on a Cornish beach
riding towards Ygraene.
Caedmon saw them: I see them:
Trees, rocks, birds, the endless rain:
Weorc wuldorfæder, halig Scyppend [2]
Works of the Maker God, Shaper of marvels.
He made me smarter than the titled fools
who watch this country grinding to its fall.
Old men still talk about the Anarchy,
when God and all the angels slept.
Time slides us back towards that nightmare.

---

[1] Paraphrasing lines translated by Charles Foulon from the *Roman de Rou*.
[2] Two Half lines from *Caedmon's Hymn*. The line that follows is a very loose translation.

Henry lost in his own schemes, his brutal sons
made war against their father for his queen.
King of everything, alone, abandoned, beaten
with nothing to cling to but his own frail bones.
 The rich make their own rules, while the law rests
at their table, yawning at atrocities.

Have you heard what happened to whatshisname?
John couldn't catch him so he locked up the wife
and eldest son and had them starved to death.
They found the mother's teeth marks in the boy.
I heard she chewed his cheeks. I remember her.
Pretty girl. Danced well. Good figure.
Nice teeth too. Could never keep her mouth shut.

So tell us stories.
A dream of heroes, as if history
could pivot on the sword arm of one man
or a single woman's beauty alter everything.
Does anyone believe Troy risked destruction
so a princeling could retain his stolen bride?
Reduce the mess that's history to fireside tales.

4

Laȝamon lithen geonde lande
During the Interdict the silence of unrung bells
was the sound God made holding His breath.
No one was married, no one was buried
and the roads weren't safe for a travelling priest

At first I scurried from library to library:
straight lines drawn from shrine to shrine
on a pilgrimage to find out more.
Searching for books, addicted to the next fact,
turning pages, mumbling words,
ignoring the irony: Geoffrey's Latin,
Wace's Frensche, the eye glides on
but catches on the thorns of Bede's Old English,
is baffled by the great book in Exeter cathedral.
Easier in French, more popular in Latin.
To tell the deeds of the English, in English.
To describe the land of the English, in English.
Hard work for little fame. Why bother?

I walked the Herepaths, soaked liked the Saxons,
saw the sleeping Kings by the still grey river
trudged the Roman roads. Those terrible straight lines
where the distance never seems to shorten.
Imagining the legions' inexorable progress.
I saw towns, battlefields, ruins, barrows.
Smouldering trace of Routier scat.
Scrape the barrel and then look under,
you'll find them. Lowlanders, lesser than beasts.
Even the dogs despise them. Knights on the move.
The dead unburied. The Churches closed.
From Tintagel to the highlands
and the strangest of all lochs. Did not,

as Wace did, hope to see fairies in the forest
was not, as he was, disappointed.

Then the tide changed: the pause, ebb, race
(I'd learnt the rule of sixths). I loved libraries.
I still do, but stayed on the road, with the tinkers,
carters, drovers, merchants and messengers.
Huddled round the fire with shepherds,
listening to the music of rough voices
passing on stories like coins worn smooth by age.
The elves that turned up for king Arthur's birth.
The king who thought that he could fly.
Sat at the lord's table, trading whatever gift was valued:
translator, reader, scribe, for a good meal
and his storytellers. I had met with learned men
envied their erudition. The herbalist who knew
the name and properties of every plant
who'd forgotten the smell of fresh turned soil
or the irritation of mud under his fingernails.
I watched the swirling patterns on the surface of the river.
Watched the sea roll in, sunlit or rain pelted

All of it *weorc wuldorfæder*.

Woke beside a girl and the glory of her at sunrise,
the fall of her breasts as she bent above me.
Wasn't her beauty also *weorc wuldorfæder*?

Sang a good song, laughed at a crude joke.
Began to wonder why life should exclude learning
or learning require I abdicate from life?

5

vppen Seuarne staþe; sel þar him þuhte.
on-fest Radestone;

Returned to this little church, surrounded by fields
redolent of cow shit, to watch the river
and serve the Lord. It's not the world's end.
There's a hermit living down at Redstone rock
where the road crosses the river on the way to Wales,
a knight who gave it all away.
Horrified by what he'd seen and done.
He tells me stories of King Stephen's day.
When God and all his angels slept.
I think they're still in hibernation.

The ferryman and I both watch the road.
He asks his fee, the hermit hopes for alms,
I ask 'what news?' Sometimes we starve.
Sometimes we glut our appetites.
A welsh knight homing from crusade.
His armour dinted, his faith glorying
in the memory of massacres.

They say that John is dead.
Rumours of another civil war.
Sons arming against fathers.
Magnates mustering their hosts.
Rumours of a French invasion
castles under siege.
They say a child frets on the throne
but the aging Marshall holds his hand.

Underneath this dented surface,
running steadily and unnoticed

local gossip, local pride.
The extraordinary lives of ordinary folk.
Make it into English. The noble deeds
of the British Kings. Ignore linguistic irony.
Ignore the little people who you live amongst.
Something tugs at me, back of the wind
the whispering thought: I want to do this
for the pleasure of its doing.

His octosyllabic couplets
in English turn problematic
and the four beat English line
is the pulse of a vanished time.
The available forms
have been gutted and bled out.
'Taste' becomes the repetition
of an unexamined inheritance
for a knowing audience.
There is no future in subservience
to the fashions of the ignorant
or the applause of pedants.
No way of knowing
what tomorrow might approve.

The word becomes flesh
and dwells in the minds of strangers.
A hand scratches across the page
and Locrin enters the earth house.
The pictures in my head
carried down the centuries
on the lips of strangers.
Is that not also *weorc wuldorfæder*?

Leave all the maps behind.
Risk the long journey out
in a fragile craft,
to a doubtful landfall.

Better to fail going out,
than live safely in the snug
reassurance of banality.
Better to live one step from success;
another from oblivion.

6

An preost wes on leodan, Laʒamon wes ihoten

God rescued us at Lincoln.
Now there is a King beneath the Law.

A dark shape, wind blown
watching the river down below
smiling at the swirling patterns
more intricate than the finest page
of an illuminated gospel.

The boy who holds his horse
tired, cold, miserable, whines
an intermittent counterpoint
to the rain scattering wind.
Behind them on the rise,
a small red church beside the yew tree,
symbol of eternity and resurrection.

Fathers

(Cornwall, a Century after the fall of Troy.)

1

Follow the wind as it tears off the Atlantic,
leaping the cliff to assault the mail clad figures.
This guard of honour, leaning against the blast.
Banners, rattling overhead, bending, threaten
to haul their shaggy bearers up into the sky

Behind them, rising in concentric rings,
the hill fort, with its palisade and tower.
On the parapet, which rattles, sways and groans
Corineus Giant-Killer, Champion, face
like a fractured cliff. Despite his age,
takes no notice of a gale. His daughter, Gwendoline
shelters in the eddy he creates, smaller, dark hair
flicking her thin face. Her wind smoothed dress
to show her heavy breasts, long legs, and sturdy thighs.
She's looking inland at the dark line, eagerly
watching as it winds over the wind-battered fields
becoming royal banners, riders, always
becoming something else.

'The confident little prick, not an outrider in sight.
Always doing the wrong thing to prove it isn't.'
'Take it as a compliment,' she gentles the rumble.
'Who'd dare attack him west of Tamar?'
But she knows there are pirates rummaging the coast,
she's seen what happens to the overconfident.
Knowing where to look she sees her father's men.
If this is not the King, the approaching column
will never reach that first embankment.
She'd seen what armies do to the defeated,
heard the women screaming while the victors ran amuck.
Don't think because she's female, young and pretty
she's not as brutal as the men she stands beside.

These people are not you in fancy dress.
Their values are not yours. Don't make that mistake.
Don't think the absence of technology means they're stupid.
You wouldn't last a month in her world.
She'd soon be running yours.

Locrin, dismounting, King of one third of the island.
The heralds do the greeting while he smiles at her.
She smiles at him. His mind slides on formalities.
His mouth moves to say appropriate words.
Thinking, such a fine young animal.
Beneath him and above him, exuberant.
She bows and greets him, her future husband.
The face, he thinks, retains its Trojan heritage
but the eyes.
He turns towards the mountain that's her father.
Corineus was daddy's darling: the man to win the war.
Giant-Killer, Town-Burner, Terror,
beloved leader of the people west of Tamar.

And there were giants in the land in those days:
incoherent lust and hunger wrapped in slabs of stinking flesh.
Stomping the green damp landscape,
before Laȝamon sang Britain into being,
naming the rivers, roads and towns,
rooting them in stories.
Before Brutus landed, last of the Trojans,
there were giants in the land in those days
until Corineus killed them all.

Locrin: the army's darling, his father's son
bred like a prize stallion, born to lead the herd.
Tall, broad-shouldered, narrow-waisted,
a marble god come down from his plinth.
She was his the day that she was born
to cement a friendship often tested, never broken.
They had played together. Learnt together.

He was her friend, she his, before they learnt to fuck.
Why should we wait he'd said,
why deny ourselves such pleasure?
She's seen him fight. He is magnificent. His father's son
fearless, bold, aggressive, swift to strike.
She watched him carve a raiding party into meat.
She lost a brother in that battle. But watching Locrin
she had been sickened by the flood of her desire.

Steering oar beneath his arm,
determined thrust of the skiff beneath his feet
vibrant, alive, an evening crossing, past familiar cliffs.
Racing for the well- known landfall
the storm outran them and exploded overhead.
Howling his exhilaration, rain smashed
wind blasted, the ship's demented rise and stall
the lurch and fall, exuberant in his defiance
until the storm's indifference
skidded him beyond control to where
endurance was his only option.

She watched him snoring on the rugs
felt the long warm stretch of him.
Such a fine young animal, so beautiful,
so distant too. She could not break through
to that place where you and I dissolve.
Framing trade as competition, not mutual generosity,
he was camped on Ictus, and she was on the beach
She could raise her hand, and touch his back,
cooler now the sweat had dried.
But the tide stayed over the causeway.

So, riddle me this, here's Locrin:
he's got everything.
His kingdom, respect, affection.
He's going to marry Gwendoline
(and there's not a straight man in the country doesn't want her):

two great families joined forever
and if you listen, you can hear Dame Fortune
click the ratchets of her wheel.

2

Domestic interior.
'So you want him, and he wants you, and married you shall be,'
the old giant-killing rock rumbles to his darling daughter.
The slaves, invisible, about their tasks. Hall-noise some way off.
'Your daughter will be queen and your grandson will be king.'
It's what he wants. Why does he pause?
                              'Brutus was my friend and Lord.
I would have died for him. But as a family, they're not good
at balancing desire and duty. Great great whatever
Paris, sold a city for a smile.'

She's heard the story many times, once, before
she'd interrupted: 'You don't think the world well lost for love?'
'Troy wasn't his to lose, what choice did he give those who died?'
'Had you been Priam, what would you have done?'
'Flogged Helen back to Sparta and sent his body with her.'

'And then there's great-great-what-not Hector,
standing to his duty. Knowing Troy will fall,
knowing his wife will be a fuck toy for the Greeks
his baby son thrown off the burning walls
to splatter on the rocks below.
Knowing he's no match for Brute Achilles
but standing to his duty all the same.
Dragged three times round the walls behind a chariot.
Or three times round a dead Greek's funeral pyre.
Gods what was left for Priam to reclaim?
They never get the balance right.
Think of great-granddaddy Aeneas.
Now there's your man for destiny and duty.
Shame about the first wife and the Queen of Carthage
the dead, unsung, unburied in his wake because his mother was a God.
Lord Pretty Boy, your lover, Locrin, has no grandfathers.

His father killed them both. One was an accident.
Perhaps. The other, well, we trashed his armies,
looted all his wealth, sailed off with his daughter
and left a hamstrung lamb to circling wolves.
I've seen the way he looks at you,
if you weren't Gwendoline I'd worry.
Love him, whatever that might mean,
honour and obey him as you should.
But if he hurts you
I will hang him by his guts.'

The messenger arrived before the dawn,
the only one surprised to find that Gwendoline
was there to hear the news: German raiders.
Locrin's brother, Alba, King of the North:
his army massacred, his head placed on a pole,
and now this German, Humber, demanding recognition.

Gwendoline watching Locrin,
enjoying the display of competence.
She saw the echoes of his father:
the way he moved amongst the council,
the direct question, the natural authority
making men eager for his notice and regard.
Gods but he was beautiful. And if
the next time that she saw him
he was a hacked beef
she would prepare the corpse for burial
and remember him like this.

But oh, my lover, sometimes
the Gordian knot will have to be unpicked.
A strong arm and a sharp sword
will be no match for a patient mind.

Of course, her father will go with him. The army love them both.
Together they will roll this Humber down into the sea.

Corineus to his daughter: 'Take the Old Guard.
Go to Ictus. Make sure the fair is a success.'
She curtseys without irony:
'There are rumours; pirates nesting in the coves.
We'll sweep them out as we go past.'
Neither man asks how she knows.
Or doubts she'll do it. Corineus has lost three sons.
All strong and brave, dying where they should,
in the front rank. But the gods rolled the dice,
and gave his daughter the family's share of brains.

The sailors who brave the crossing seeking tin
are welcomed by Gwendoline, who listens to their stories.
The rules are simple: information given now
will be rewarded; friendships established now
will accumulate interest 'til they return.

The merchants trust her word, her hospitality
the fairness of her judgements.
So it's easy to find an island of the dead
a place that shipmen use as shelter
easy to ask them for a simple favour.

3

How arbitrary the world
or how inexorable is wyrd.
Take your pick. Consider:

A town beside a river, the hill behind,
spotted with corpses.
The ugly sounds of victory.
The enemy in flight, the victors
flushed with adrenaline and relief
hunting down the few survivors.
Desperate men racing between the burning buildings
looking backwards as they run
for the safety of their ships

The raiders' boats already burning.
Four men jump the gunwale
mindless, freed of fear, alive
registering the smell of bilge water,
the rocking of the boat,
ripping open the tent stretched over the stepped mast:
find three women: a princess and her maids.

Pause.

How arbitrary or how fated? Take your pick.

These are predators with appetite and instinct.
Long before history drew its fragile line
between bestial and human.
What should happen next:
they rape the women, slit their throats
then plunder the treasure scattered through the ship.
But these four men.

These four men take the princess and her maids
unharmed, to the King.
Hurrying through the wash of voices,
fending off anyone who tries to intervene.
Why?
Because, if you listen carefully
you can hear that ratchet click.

Locrin, watching a line of prisoners waiting for the axe,
the scop naming the dead, naming the deserving.
He is thinking soon he can ride west.
Soon Gwendoline will be his, every night
her brain and body at his beck and call.
He is smiling when he looks up at the golden woman.

What did he see?

Was she so beautiful she cut the thread
that tethers common sense?
She looks up at the man who'll rape her first
leaning into whatever happens next.
But the King is reaching out his open hand
saying words neither of them understand:

*sel þe scale iwurÞen wifmon þu art hende
& ic þe will habben mid wurðscipen hæʒe
to richen are queen þe ic libbe
oþer null ic habben* [3]

A building: shadows, jumbled furniture.
He takes her inside. The warriors look away.
The King is busy.

That night the golden woman sits beside the King
(Corineus is chasing down survivors)
simple but effective sign for people trained to notice.

---
[3] Locrin's first speech to Aestrild in the *Brut*.

Not at his feet, a concubine to use and then discard
but level with him with her hand in his.
His ring on a gold chain around her neck.
The solid world begins to turn to water:
                                        Click, click click
She sleeps beside him, trussed and tethered to a stake
so she can't run or shank him while he snores.

The river was the loudest noise he'd ever heard
far louder than the noise of armies when they clash.
He'd tried to follow it upstream.
For years now, this same recurring dream:
smooth spray drenched boulders
piled against the sheer walls of the gorge
brambles capable of tearing bronze.

He moves so slowly and so painfully
moving her shift off her shoulders
finest cloth on the whitest skin he's ever seen.
Clouds sliding off the moon
his hands on her breasts.
As the cloth falls, he falls
for the first time into the river
weightless, free
cradled by the current moving to the sea.

The violence clatters on outside
inside the benches scattered
blood spatters on the floor
the table thrown against the wall.
She stands against it,
there is nowhere else to go.
Like dust motes in the light
that streams in through smashed timber
silence flows from her.
She does not move, or plead, or beg.
She stands to meet whatever happens next head on.

A sharp intake of breath,
a tremor willed to stillness
and nothing else.

He's heard the old men talk
of marble statues in Troy's vanished halls.
If he had seen one, he would know,
exactly what she would remind him of.
His weather-tarnished hands remove her shift.
He thinks of shadows moving over whitest cliffs.
Her skin so white. Her shift was falling
He was falling:
Click click click

4

File it under stories told about his father.
The island was a wooded hill
rising sharply to a barren ridge.
A colony had squeezed itself
between the shoreline and the trees.
The wall was broken, buildings burnt
a scattering of bone and rags
scat of raiders from the sea.
On the slopes, a sacred grove
thick trees older than the gods
trees that had waited for the first man
given shelter to the first birth
thick horizontal branches
scoured by the hangman's rope.
Tumbled stones, split by their roots
caked in the blood of sacrifice.
At the centre, incongruous, a statue:
Diana, virgin huntress, flanked by lions
polished by the wind and rain.

Brutus chose three captives:
young, strong, unblemished.
Strung them from the sacred tree and cut them open
Poured their blood over the statue
Stroked it, kissed it, uttered invocations.
Asked his questions. Waited.

Dark rose in the sacred grove
A night wind swung the hanging forms.
The swarming flies rose and settled rose and settled.
The wood groaned.
The ropes sang. The lions stretched
and growled. The bloody goddess

stepped down from her plinth.
'Oh cowering man, oh fearful, shaking man
take your fleet of hollowed ships
west into the raging swirl of Ocean.
There is an island to the north.
There is fish and game and
the green fields are fertile.
Land where the coast is red.
It will be yours and your descendants'
If you will worship me.'
The goddess stooped to kiss the man
and made the night implode.

Now Locrin understood
Marble. Statue. Adoration
A sideways movement out of time.
Out of himself as she backed against the table.

Incongruous grace amidst the carnage
A marble statue of Diana, virgin huntress
polished by the rain.
'The devil's concubine' spits our Christian Poet
but his hero stopped to worship her
white wraith in his dreams
exquisite dream-sex
promising him this kingdom.

'Have you come to take it back?'
Incongruous beauty amidst the carnage.
'Or ratify the promise in the daylight.'

Locrin on a rock dispensing gifts.
The pile of treasures, the line of captive women.
The four men who bought her to him
lavished with estates.
Grumbling amongst the ranks:
were these first at the breaking of shields?

What did they do in the battle?
Things no one dares say aloud.
They still trust Locrin.

The massed spears wave erratically.
A gale is blowing through the forest,
parting the lines. Corineus with his axe
bellowing in rage, striding towards the King
and look, even Locrin's bodyguard
who would die for him
sway back before that axe.

'Nithing', he is howling, 'Nithing!
You have betrayed my daughter.
You have insulted me.
Brutus was not your father,
your mother was a whore who screwed a swineherd.
No son of my old friend would shame me thus.
For this golden slit you spurn my daughter.
Is this how you repay me?
You do not know who she is, or where she's from,
her parents or her family. Nithing!
You do not even know her name!'

Locrin leans into this gale that sweeps towards him.
As the old giant killing axe begins to fall
thought fluttering: he's right, I will die
and I don't know her name.

The axe smashes down into the rock.
The rock he's standing on.
The rock splits.

In winter the Atlantic gales
drag the grey sea, raging
and throw it at the cliffs for days.
Rage will carry him no further.
He will not kill his best friend's son.

The guards move, the Witan cluster,
speeches are made, bargains sought.
The army will not have their darlings at each other's throats.
It takes all day. Locrin will marry Gwendoline.
They will drown the foreign witch
whose magic overpowered his reason.
They will not fight a war for this.

The earl looks baffled, kneels.
'My Lords, the witch has disappeared.
We found the maids, both dead
but the witch has gone.'

Corineus was not born yesterday.
He no longer trusts Lord Pretty Boy.
His men return, report the woman gone.

5

There will be a wedding.
Her gift to him: The statue of Diana,
Gwendoline paid its weight in tin.
She stares at it and wonders,
did Helen look like this?
And if she did, how was she worth Troy's walls?

Close-cropped hair, a child's breasts and legs,
this is no goddess: more adolescent boy than girl.
A man's ideal of woman. It's never quiet when he's loud
or happy when he's sad, always instantly available
aroused when he is, or surplus to requirements when he's not.
There are no edges, no complexities, no awkwardness.
Brutus loved her island, its rough edges and harsh corners
the sandbanks, shoals and shallows guarding her approaches.
So much more interesting than a dreamy promise of perfection.
The virgin hunter, who protects the game she kills.
Goddess of unmarried girls: Goddess of childbirth.
Truth lies in paradox; knowledge in teasing out her contradictions.

Locrin, baffled,
trying not to hurt his friend,
knowing she has made the effort.
So this is marble?
(But this can't be the statue
It doesn't look like her.)

Brutus, standing in the gateway
watching the Cornish retinue recede.
There are two types of queen,
he said, surprising Locrin.
A brood mare for the bloodline
or a loyal friend at the council.

The second's rare, but there's a fabled third
who is both, and loving of her Lord.
He nodded to the banners.
You are the Lucky Man. Gods rolls the dice,
who understands why they should fall the way they do?

The warband, guaranteed to spread the news:
Witchcraft! Of course,
he was bewitched: those evil foreign girls.

Locrin, days after the battle, lying beside Gwendoline.
'She was no witch. I thought she was Diana,
come to ratify the bargain in the daylight.'
'It is a necessary lie…'
                        'King's don't lie.'
'Then tell the host you broke your oath
admit that you betrayed their darling
went back on your father's promise to Corineus and me.
For what? They die upon your word.
Do you think they'd do that for someone they can't trust?
Tell them she was a witch. It's easy to believe.
Who'd think you'd risk your kingdom for a girl.'
He says, 'A king may keep a concubine',
aware his statement sounds like a request.
'Call her what you will.
A king can have as many heifers in his herd
as lust and greed can service
but there can only be one Queen.'

Exterior. Ramparts. Some days after the wedding.
Distant sounds of happy celebrations.
Locrin watching the autumn landscape
noticing the feminine curve of the hills.
The smell of night stinging his nostrils.
Dark rising from the ripples in the ground
to spread the sun as it fades.
Night, closing the book.

The sleeper safe in the dark.
The watching set to the vigil.
The stillness; the sense of calm
the peace of sleep.
Peace for the watchful, an end to slaughter.
A bench scrapes in the stillness.
The clouds fall off the moon.

'They're singing songs about our fathers.'
      'I've heard them all before.
Tomorrow I will publicly give thanks,
officiate at the offerings
ask for forgiveness for my sins
praise the Gods for our victory
and the beauty of your smile.'

She quotes his father, not hers
Ic tō sōþe wāt
þæt biþ in eorle   indryhten þēaw
þæt hē his ferðlocan   fæste binde,
healde his hordcofan, hycge swā hē wille. [4]

He laughs, translating the too familiar maxim:
'It is a noble custom for a man to keep his mouth shut?'
And she too laughs, watchful,
trying to steer him from disaster:
'A king who prays in public lies to his gods.
His earls must never know the secrets of his heart.
If he is honest: he gives them hostages.
If discrete; he offends the gods.
So officiate at the rituals of thanks
but say your prayers in private.'

[Sometimes I look at you and I'm afraid:
so clever and so self-contained.
The glare of your ferocious competence

---

[4] From 'The Wanderer'.

illuminates how fragile I can feel.
I look for tenderness, affection, even honesty.
Instead you lie for both of us,
pretending I'm the man you want
when you're so wedded to perfection
I'm just another test of excellence.]

'Then I will go to Troy Nouvante,
rebuild the temple of Diana
and pray there, fasting, for a week alone,
perform the rituals, ask her forgiveness,
for we who have forgotten her.'

6

Night, the cold dark, his clothes soaked.
To his left; the persistent bloated river
hurrying past, To his right; the ridge
rising, like a shadow on the wall of darkness.
No stars, only the darker folding of the clouds
the guide certain, the torch inadequate
his horse stumbles, finding its feet,
complains.

Build me an earth house hidden away.
Make the doors of whalebone.
Guard her well and hide her there.

He would keep her safe until
he could return her to her country
with gold and rings
befitting the daughter of a king.

Build me an earth house.
They had found a hidden cave.
'A man should always do his lord's behest
even when he knows it's wrong.'
Our Poet's strangest comment, if it's not ironic.

Dark rider on the riverbank at dusk,
he can smell how cold the water is.
Listening to it hurry past, a pale stain
between the overhanging trees.
A whale bone door in the cliff face,
a stale moon behind sick clouds.
The flickering army on the other bank
dead ancestors, mustering against his crossing.
Go forward or go back? Dame Fortune

cranked her wheel to bring him here,
and being here means everything has changed.
Better to die knowing than on the frontier of a mystery?

He stood outside the cave door.
He would send her home,
with gold and rings.
But the daughter of a dead king
becomes a mattress for the unworthy.[5]
She would be safer here.

If only he could meet himself going in and coming out
and ask, well, was she worth it?

Candle light, grave yard smell of the dank earth
damp stone and wooden roof supports.
Smell of perfume burning in the brazier.
She has counted out the weeks.
The way she will count the months and then the years.
Her maids are mute; the guards say nothing.
They take her out to ride at night along the river.
No one smiles. No one speaks.
In the depths of a mountain pass,
on the coldest night of the year,
the silence is less complete.

A woman staring at her fire.
We see her from behind.
Then her face, in profile
as an unexpected sound
snaps the ritual silence.
The tall man straightens entering the cave,
moves towards her with such clumsy haste
she hears things breaking in his wake,
the great doors being closed.

---

[5] This is a variation on López d'Aguirre's reported comment that he shot his daughter to prevent her becoming 'a mattress for the unworthy'.

The servants and the guards are gone.
His good intentions swept away
in the flood of desperation,
until, exhausted, she curls into him.
One calloused hand cupping the fluid marvel of her breast,
the long cool length of her against him,
her golden hair across the furs.

7

They do not argue, Locrin and his Queen:
she tortures him with patient explanations.
'You do not breed a stallion to pull a merchant's cart.
It carries heroes into battle.' 'Peace,' she says,
'is the farmer going to his field without fear
expecting to benefit from his labour,
his buildings unburnt, his family alive at harvest time.
It is to act as though there is a law and consequence.
Prosperity is trade: the ship safe to the harbour,
eager men shifting goods along safe roads
to predictable protected fairs.'
                              'There's precious little
glory in all your Peace', he says and she agrees but adds:
'The sheep will always need a shepherd.'
'But no sheep ever sang the shepherd's praise.'

The banner stutters on the hill.
The wall of shields around it dark,
darker, darkening.
Locrin slaughtering his way towards it.
He is not alive, but life itself, not strong, but strength;
vigorous, exuberant, vibrant. He's never felt so good
the dull collision of his axe against bronze shield,
the jarring wrench as blade encounters bone;
nothing. He grows in strength with every man he kills
as though their lives are added to his own.

But the tumbling bodies form a wall
that builds itself around the banner.
He clambers up, unhindered by dead hands,
slithering but killing as he goes.

Even in this dream he knows,
the only way he'll reach it is to stop.
But if he stops he dies.
And so the dead accumulate,
while the banner stutters in the fading light.

In a world where every journey requires a conscious effort
the ease of this one takes him by surprise.
From admiration to contempt:
a swift, unnoticed crossing.
Desire to disgust.
The qualities that fascinated
become the flicking of a blade.
The sight and sound of Gwendoline
a bitter poison until
he flinched when someone spoke her name.

8

When Locrin was still honest
he trusted words like loyalty and truth.
Now he sees potential liars everywhere.
The men who guard her swear an oath:
he hears sounds fading in the air.
'Give me five years of your life,' he says.
(The old man can't live much longer.)
'And I will give you fabulous estates and wealthy wives
for now, take gold rings, armlets
the best of horses, jewel encrusted things,
women for your pleasure, I will make you rich.'
They will be so wealthy that they can't be bribed.
Whatever they desire, he will provide.
So they become the keepers of his prison
and he must flatter men he would despise.

I thought she was Diana
come to ratify her gift.
'Or take it back?'

His golden insanity.
Why was the lie so easy to repeat?
Because he was praying,
in a rite, rich with personal significance.
So utterly lost he thinks
he is the man he wants to be,
with a woman who can't speak his name.

Blue eyes in the candlelight,
white skin, golden hair.
Locrin on his knees, praying for oblivion.
Lying nestled into her,
the length of flesh against flesh.

Exhausted, wondering, why?
This mute Rapunzel in her tower.
Tomorrow or the next day he will think,
why risk all this? This being everything
beyond the catalogue, beyond the reach of any map
or circumnavigation.

He wanders through the empty halls.
Finds no one in this ruined memory of Troy.
Even the echoes of the terrified have faded.

Brutus was not the kind of man who'd teach his son;
dispensing advice the way he might distribute
plunder to a war band. Rare enigmatic speech
that might be wisdom, ransacked from experience
long considered, or just the sudden need
to hear his own voice. Last of the Trojans.
His past was legend locked inside a walled enclosure:
all those mutilated ghosts demanding proper burial
clamouring for retribution.

And every man will stand before his parents' graves
framing the questions he should have asked
when they could choose to answer:

How did it feel to kill your father?
Did it make you free: no promise to fulfil?
No old men telling you how daddy would have done it?
Your grandfather went to hell to get his father's blessing.
I'd never go that far. But how can I compete with what you did?
Where is the glory in her world of farmers, trade and litigation?

And mother, then a maiden, stripped and offered to a stranger.
Your wedding night a bruising nightmare orchestrated
by your frightened father who bought his freedom
from the violent, silent man he gave you to.
One warm soft piece of payment perched

naked, on a pile of cold and burnished plunder.
Carted to the waiting ships. They say,
watching from the stern, you wept for days
as your country faded to a stain on the horizon.
They also say my father tried to comfort you.
I want to ask now if that story's true.
It doesn't sound like something he would do.

The day after tomorrow, or the night after that
lying beside his wife, desire for the other
creeps back into his bed, soft fingers becoming claws
dragging him towards the earth house in his dreams.

9

Gwendoline, pregnant
flicking words like little knives
not caring if he bleeds.
Rarely, it gentles her edges.
She looks without assessing him
a rare softness in his arms:
affection without question marks.
Then he tells himself never again.
I will not risk this.
Never again. That time was the last
I will send men to take her home
with gifts, with wealth, with honour.
But I must see her first, explain.

Aestrild, pregnant
careful and slow, more watchful,
sinking into a smiling silence
as he strokes the life growing inside her.
Her face on the pillow beside him
most beautiful of sights.
Waking beside her, as she shifts into wakefulness
holding her as the sun rises,
where they have escaped from the earth house
to the riverbank in spring,
he wants for nothing.
Wondering, this sense of wonder could be mine.

What difference to her life
if her father were alive?
He'd dangle her in front
of every princeling who came courting.
Prize mare for the loudest stallion

who'd toss her when her beauty fades.
No, this was better, she was safer here with him

Locrin stumbles through Troy's ransacked halls
hunting the ghost of Paris to demand an answer:
'Was Helen worth the death of Troy?'
Screams still fading in the clash of bronze.
In roofless buildings where ghosts are mangled by the wind
he stumbles on the debris, startled by a movement,
stands on Troy's smashed walls, where Priam sat
watching death creep closer, year by bloody year,
to everyone he loved and promised to defend.
Dry wind comes off the plain with sounds of distant horses
though the coast is clear, the stars still imitate their fires
but the Greeks have gone, the gods have gone
and there's no more heroes left to claim a song.

10

Locrin's devotion to Diana ensures the Kingdom is at peace.
With no fighting to be done, he turns to prayer
and supervising the rebuilding of her temples.
 Gwendoline runs the kingdom while he's gone.
When he's there, protocol demands
the supplicant address the King.
If he were more attentive he would see
the covert way they watch his Queen.

Who is no fool. But he's her husband;
her King; he was her closest friend.
She cannot bring herself to spy on him.

He often stares into the distance
like the watchmen on Ictus,
staring over the blank ocean for the first ships of the season.
She builds against whatever's coming
picks out the best and draws them to her.
Listens, pays attention, is honest and reliable
until men say the Queen's word is treasure in the hand.
Hill forts west of Tamar are rebuilt.
Alliances are made. Some people disappear.
A few dead bodies turn up now and then.

Two women.
Much the same pleasure;
much the same pain.
To Gwendoline a baby boy, of course,
to the army's joy, a future King,
called Madan.
To Aestrild, in secrecy, a daughter,
Abren. 'Most beautiful of all children' says the Poet.

The boy soon goes to Cornwall with a wet nurse.
Safe from palace intrigues and his granddaddy
will teach him well. Tell him stories of the good old days
when giants went fee fie fo fum and had their heads crushed
by the same big hands that bounce his little Lordship.

Locrin is more distant than his father was.
The squalling shitting bundle fills him with disgust.
The squalling shitting bundle in the cave's
a source of endless wonder. He holds her,
rocking gently while her mother sleeps.

The Cornish Earl arrived to tell the Queen
her father wouldn't last another month.
'Go, go,' said Locrin, 'make your peace before he dies.
Don't leave yourself as I did, burdened
with the words you wished you'd said.'

They haven't spoken for some time. She pauses.
These are the last words she will hear him say.
She wants to close the distance, hold him and be held,
find the children they had been.
Once he had been her closest friend.
But the tide's over that causeway and it's not going out.
He wishes her Godspeed and spurns the room.

Soon after she had left, taking her guard,
another messenger arrived. That secret, well-paid man
who could be trusted regardless of the task
who'd flogged his horse to bring the King the words
he longed to hear. 'My Lord, he's dead.'
Corineus, the Army's Darling, Killer of Giants, Sacker of Cities
grandfather to the heir apparent, had died in his sleep.
Locrin told his herald to find Gwendoline
but to wait 'til she had crossed the Tamar
before delivering the message:

'There can only be one queen. Stay west of Tamar.'

11

Aestrild on the throne, the silent golden beauty
a stillness in the flood of voices
like a statue in a river.
The loyal warriors murmur:
Why would the King prefer her to the Queen?

Gwendoline was her father's daughter:
no wilting wall flower she.
She heard the golden woman was called Queen.
She heard about the daughter, how the King
was doting on them both.
Calling in her debts, she mustered Cornwall,
and moved her army east, crossing the Tamar
keeping them in check. Not a farm was burnt
not a man nor woman harmed.
Her army grew; moved unmolested.
Knowing Locrin would move quickly when he moved,
tear himself from his golden wife,
lead the young men
be the army's darling once again.
The simplicity of war he understood.

She drew her army up, a forest on her left,
along a ridge that fell towards a river on her right.
She knew he wouldn't wait. No heralds, no negotiation.
The armies lined up face to face. Expect no quarter:
take no prisoners. Bring me his head, she said.
Bring me her head, he said. Do what you will first,
but bring me her head.

Her banner in the centre, dark on the afternoon sky.
The youngest men, eager for glory, knowing she was watching,
sent to crash into his wall of shields.

A mailed army on the run down slope, thrumming the ground,
the scattered cries, the sudden shock as shield encountered shield
and the awful muffled shoving match began.

Easy to pick him out, the family's plumed helmet,
sunlight flashing off his gold rimmed shield;
like a windblown firestorm flaring through tall timber.

See the men of Cornwall break and fall before him.
His warband, shields locked and spears levelled,
sweeping through the scattered debris.

The Brute Achilles back to rage towards the banner on the hill,
which darkens as the daylight starts to fade.

The young man she had picked to lead her bodyguard;
loyal, courageous, infatuated, says:
'My lady, we can get you out to safety.'
She stops herself from smiling; asks,
'Do you trust me?' He flinches as if speared.
'You need to ask?' 'Be patient.'

The plumed helmet moving closer
The boy returns, again: 'My lady
if he breaks the line
we cannot guarantee your safety.'
To his surprise, she kisses him.
Her forehead against his, breath on his sweaty face.
'Be patient. After we have won this battle
I will give you lands, I will sing the praises
of your skill and courage. I will repay you
with wealth and honour. But
be patient, hold the line. The day is ours.'

This is the only witchcraft worth the name.
This ability to make another trust his life
to her word. To know the battle lost and think it won

because of what she says. She watches him run back
to the waving spears and ringing screams.

But Locrin, had you paid attention
to those stories old men told about your daddy
you'd know what happens next.

The day our fathers trashed the King of France,
they were outnumbered. Brutus held the centre.
They said that Hector and Aeneas fought beside him,
while Corineus waited in the trees with half the army
until the time was ripe, and when the time was ripe
they came and smashed into the French king's flank.
You knew that columns crumple if taken from the right?

You do now.

The veterans of her father's guard, men who knew wisdom,
some she'd known all her life, who wouldn't say
'we love you as our daughter' but thought it just the same,
who would die before anyone could harm the daughter of Corineus,
came out of the trees and smashed into the shoving column.
The right-hand side, the side where no shields were.

He stood his ground, knowing this was worth a song,
heaping the dead around the swaying plumes.

Locrin's army slaughtered, the river running red.
Locrin among the scattered bodies, shot by arrows.
They brought her Locrin's head as she requested.
She did not wash the blood with tears,
she did not kiss the broken mouth or spit on it.
She nodded, gave proof of thanks to thanes,
ordered it be buried with respect.
If nothing else he was the bravest of all men.

12

They brought the woman and her whelp.
Oh she had planned her punishment
so vile the stones would melt
before they were forgotten.
But she looks up and meets her eyes.

One time Gwendoline had gone to Ictus
she had braved the mother barrow in the night.
Her father had slain giants, but the shape unnerved her;
a recumbent she, dilating before birth, the dark slit
of the passageway leading down towards nothing
and the nothing was darker and quieter
than darkness and silence.

She saw that Aestrild was behind that nothing now.
All those years of silence underground,
taken out for exercise like a mare
perfumed and pampered
waiting for the stallion's visit:
the regular, repeated rape.

Sees neither witch nor goddess
just a shattered woman with her child
leaning into the inevitable.
Choice is a luxury commodity
which belongs to those with wealth and power.
What choice did Aestrild ever have?
The council can decide.
'What is the punishment for witchcraft?'

They tie the two together and toss them in the river,
mother and child, in the current running red,
and if the tide returns them, later

weeks or months, to any beach
then anyone who finds them
will not think them worth a kingdom.

Gwendoline and her captains walk amongst the dead.
No nightmare this of rising ground fog
just a field of grass with tumbled bodies,
some still dying.

For the first time, Gwendoline weeps,
for young men dead and women grieving.
She makes a promise to her thanes
(The Queen's word is a treasure in your hand):
she will rule until her son is old enough.
She will rule so that a woman, with a baby at her breast,
or a man, with the red gold in his bag,
could walk the length of Britain unmolested.
And that, says La3amon, is what she did
retiring to Cornwall, to the joy of her people,
when her son was old enough to rule.

Interlude number two: two stories from Bede

1) Recovering Oswald's relics

The morning opens on to desperate riders.
Avoiding the road, infrequent farms,
the explosive betrayal of startled dogs
they reach this famous place of slaughter
deep in the landscapes of their enemy
where the grass is greener for the blood-soaked soil
on the humped mound where the victors mourned their dead.
Scattered bones of the defeated litter the field
and the impaled heads nod to the ground
on their listing poles. A year after the battle
they seek one skull amongst so many.

Perception hinged on a swinging sword;
as the skull split live king became dead saint
at that moment of complete despair
before Penda raged unchallenged through the north.
A startled raven helps them with the arm and hand.
It flusters up into a tree, then drops an arm:
a spring erupts beneath it where it lands.

Avoiding roads, infrequent farms, they outrun everything,
to bring the relics home.

2) The Death of King Sigbert of East Anglia

The armoured men beyond the wall
wait in the simplicity of their need.
Day fading into frigid dusk, still not one
speaks even when the great gate opens
and from the torches and the crowd
a monk steps out towards them.

They know his broken nose, his greying beard.
They recognize the hands that carved their enemies.
That voice of absolute command. He knows them all.
You were there when I renounced the kingdom.
You were there when I took holy vows
You were witnesses to my decision.
Why trouble me?

            When you were king
nobody troubled us. Now Penda burns our halls.

I cannot lead you into battle.
I have renounced the sword.
I grow herbs in the garden.
I watch the river rise and fall.
You can kill me here.
I will not fight with you.

They flinch at his simplicity,
at the thought of this great warrior growing weeds.
But they have not come to be refused.
Awkward in their violent deference,
they bundle him on to a horse
and ride towards their camp.

The army cheers full-throated welcome
with the old King looking on it cannot lose.
His nobles offered him his sword and he refused.
He refused mail and shield, but took a stick
and found his place beside the royal banner.
How simple to believe he could escape to silence
or evade the choices that his parents made.
From the day that he was born this death was waiting for him
the pole as yet unsharpened for his desecrated corpse.

He did not live to see his army scattered.
His thanes, so certain of his magic presence,
did not live to reproach him for their failure.
They lie scattered on the trodden grass
under the shut eyed stare of his severed head.
The herbs will grow without him.
Someone else is free to water them
and watch the river rise and fall.

Fragments from
The Fall of Britain

Memorial Stone

(Western Britain, late fourth century AD)

Blank, from the something legion?
Erected by, I'm guessing here, his wife?

1

The Successful Man
(late fourth century)

The way you hold your hand,
like this,
reveals the fine imported cloth along your sleeve
and draws attention to the mosaic floor,
the hypocaust, the bath house;
the roses you brought all the way from Gaul,
the library, 'expensive, but essential,
where would we be without our poets?'
The wife whose pedigree's beyond reproach.
(Perhaps your Roman guests will laugh
behind your back, 'She's so provincial'
but her jewels will dazzle them).
Armed thugs 'to keep the scum in line',
slaves who greet your guests
will later pander to their private greeds.

Your guided tours omit to name
the dead, the disappointed and betrayed;
old friends you left beyond the Wall.
The price those nameless others paid
so you could ape the Roman lord
in townhouse, villa and estate.

2

The Landowner
(circa 400 AD)

The first incomers that we met?
Perhaps two families;
birds out of season on a barren field
scratching a bit of land nobody wanted.
Nothing to sell, too poor to trade.
We did not offer them advice or aid.
Planted late their crops all failed.
When winter started, they began to starve.

A dumb show in the doorway:
a pregnant girl in rags against the cold
another, tall, erect, but clothed in filth
four dirt creased shrivelled claws
opened, shaking, reaching up for food.
We beat them to the boundaries.
When their men did not come,
armed against the insult,
we called our neighbours,
took up weapons, killed them all.

The Friesian Coast
(winter, 409 AD)

On the edge of this flat land
sky and sea can be confused.
Gaze slides over surface
snagging on a clump
of wind-stripped grass,
almost missing ships
hauled above high water
hummocked under snow
and the wind rattled shanties
scattered though the dunes.

Here men gather
in the long winter, in the stale
smoked fug of themselves,
talk, boast, bicker
watching the grey,
snow-crusted waves
slushing the beach.

The heroic past has faded into poetry.
Their fathers' stories
will not keep them fed or warm.

This man has lost his family and his farm.
This one fought for Rome, or so he says.
The quiet boy is running from the fear
he will become his father. They say
this man has raided down the Saxon Shore.

But a shield and a spear
earns a place at the oars.
A willingness to die
pays long odds on a future.

4

Oral History
(*mid fifth century*)

My granny saw the last Roman Galley
slipping down the Solent. She'd seen
the fleet go out before, it was nothing strange.
There was nothing memorable about the day:
it was a grey day, clouds, no wind. No time to gawk.
And anyway, no reason to. It was nothing strange
to see the fleet shrink towards the open sea.

5

The End of a Roman's Britain
(*early fifth century*)

'We waited for the tax collectors
on the appointed day,
shuffling our seasonal excuses,
banquet and bribes prepared
to damp the threat behind the smile.
Growing impatient, we watched the road
cautiously going about our lives
waiting for their trap to shut.

Whisperings across the fields:
the Legions have gone over
they've left us on our own.
My neighbour celebrated, caring only
that bribes and banquet were not wasted.

My wife and daughters
demanded that we leave.
They'd heard the stories.
Attacotti eat the flesh
of living victims.
Preferable to what Germani
do with captive women.
The silver that I'd stashed
would buy us passage.
We could start again.
But I'd heard the Rhine
was breached. Goths
were marching towards Rome.
When the world is coming to an end
there's nowhere safe to 'start again'.

Here on the bench seat in my garden
in the fragrant twilight, thinking:
if right depends upon a sword,
there is no future in refinement.
Is life not worth the loss of leisure
my hoarded silver better spent
on foederati? My daughters
mated with their stinking leaders?'

7

Bagaudae

They naturalised their own brutality
by pointing to the letters of The Law.
It was The Law that was to blame;
not the Magistrate who sentenced,
the scribe who wrote it out, the spy,
the torturer, the executioner – The Law.
The smith who made the brand for runaways
who never smelt their burning flesh;
the carpenter who made the rack
who never heard the screams; the soldiers
who pillaged, murdered, raped and maimed
and did it with the blessing of The Law.

A whispering across the fields.
The legions have gone over and they've left us on our own.
Now the law was only what it ever was:
words wrapped around a swinging fist.

One day our master screamed:
'You are my dogs, you will obey. You know the law'
and snapped the chains of our obedience.

We nailed him to his door
where he could watch us
with his women and his wine.
When no one came to punish us
we knew we had become The Law.

8

The young men's story

Daring the unfamiliar coast
some went down with all hands,
some swift currents swept
on a shore with no shelter
some wrecked to discover
banks and shoals for those who followed.
Some were swept forever west,
to life or death, dry or drowning
no one knows.
Others braved the storms
to make safe landfall, gave thanks
sailed up streams, rolled the dice.

What you call silence
is a constellation of smaller sounds:
like stars contradicting *darkness*.

They struggled their ship
up the narrowing channel
cursing the headwind
cursing the shallows
so focussed he could hear
beyond the grinding of the thole pins
beyond the water on the hull
an ant crawling in the grass
before one small sound
exploded to cacophony.
Arrow flight and spear fall
distinguished by tonalities
of impact in water, body, board and timber
before the locals carved his corpse

left heart and limbs along the river bank:
set his skull upon a sharpened stick,
facing the way he'd come.

10

Old scores

The percussive sounds of barking dogs
and in the morning, we few creeping back
to salvage and move on. Move anywhere.
Too scared to give the dead their proper rites.
Brigantes, Atrebates, Cats, all on the hunt;
hired foreign muscle settling old scores.

West Stow
(410 AD)

One day dad's family headed to the nearest town.
Tired of watching. Tired of waiting to be asked;
what will you pay us to be left alone?
There were walls and armed men on the prowl.
A shanty in a wrecked basilica.
One day 'We can't eat roof tiles',
so off we went. Dad found this place
with clear views all around
and here we stopped.
When the incomers arrived,
dad said, 'Look: we fight, the loser dies,
the winner struggles to survive.
Together, we can work this place.'

There was a boy. Hard working lad
could turn wood into anything.
Mam said, 'Don't matter where he's from
as long as he looks after you.'
Nu he bith min ceorl. Ic beo his wif
and when crops and babies came,
everyone was happy.

Oral History #2
(circa 430 AD)

My father said his grandfather,
stick fragile but persistent,
still helped around the farm
when he was in his eighties.
He'd tell my father stories:
about mere-wives in the fens,
and his adventures as a boy
in a clean and thriving city.

He'd seen the folk under the hill
riding past, intent on mischief,
and workers building houses,
fixing roofs. Been to the baths,
chased from the amphitheatre
by irate slaves whose sole task
was to sweep it clean.
He'd often seen the wild hunt

roaring through the clouds
and rows of pots for sale
coins fresh minted and unclipped
soldiers stepping along streets
that weren't clogged with rubble
and the ghosts of the Iceni
screaming for revenge.

13

Foederati
(*Kent, 450 AD*)

We fought their enemies. We kept them safe
for a tenth of the plunder and our place at the feast.
We buried our dead and told stories of home
about a long winter and the killing in spring
until Hengist called, 'silence!' Waited, then asked:
'Why do we settle for so very little?'

14

The Matter of Britain
(*Western Britain, 450 AD*)

Mog the Magnificent
in his daub and wattle hut
lord of the scattered rocks
and the wind scarped ridge
watching the sheep he's counted
penned on the wet hillside.
The members of his retinue
huddled round the fire,
dozing. The harper
droning stories of Vortigern
Hengist and Rowena.

They say it's easier to look into the sun
Than look at her. They say,
she is the dawn and when she rises day begins.

Vortigern, traitor,
expert in evil,
skilled in deceit
sold his country
for a pagan witch.

Hengist, a cunning man,
a secret, silent, scheming
man, who pimped
his daughter for a crown
he could have seized.

But I was there when Rowena walked into the hall.
She lifted up the goblet, 'Wes þu hal, Vortigern cyning'

*and I swear, Hengist had pitched her at the son
at Vortimer. She swerved. She chose
and with that choice swerved history and Britain fell.*

15

Lament for the Colonisers
(*n.d.*)

When a people are nostalgic
for brutal unembarrassed tyranny
it's clear how ugly life's become.
Everything measured,
trim, straight, squared
whips regulation length
stepping out of line
a short and bloody crawl
towards an unmarked grave.

'But we went to sleep
assuming friends would be alive
come morning and we
would be alive to greet them.'

Coda:
Presentment of Englishry

(Mumchancing it, while the question takes a hike
past dark satanic mills and pleasant (Enclosed) pastures
where we do tug a forelock as m'lady rides to hounds.
Us folks below the stairs do know our place,
stunned in the underground while bombs fall overhead.

We stood our ground at Ethendun, Stamford Bridge and Senlac hill
then bartered, buggered, battered ground into the soil
from Agincourt to Waterloo; we fell in well-drilled rows
in Somme slime screaming there is a corner of some foreign
field that is forever foreign. Smashed scorched and sunk
for Drake to Jellicoe. Hatred handed down amongst the people
we defeated, and we reviled by those we did the fighting for.

Prosperity rode misery to market, past sullen tenements
street maggot urchins breeding in the gutters while
the gin-sunk stench of slack jawed women at the gallows
slumping towards oblivion, transported, (not to joy) their men folk
beaten dogs, looking anywhere but up. By what grounds English?
West Midlands, I. Not mercenary, prat, a Mercian! Of Penda's folk.)

Gehyrest þu?

Notes on the Text

An preost wes on leoden; La3amon wes ihoten.
he wes Leouenaðes sone; liðe him beo Drihten.
He wonede at Ernle3e; at æðelen are chirechen.
vppen Seuarne stape; sel þar him þuhte.
on-fest Radestone; þer he bock radde.
Hit com him on mode; & on his mern þonke.
þet he wolde of Engle; þa æðelæn tellen.
                (La3amon's *Brut*, Lines 1-7)

There was a priest amongst the people, called La3amon (he was Leouenað's son, may the Lord be kind to him). He lived at Areley, at the noble church on the banks of the Severn. He thought it was good there, not far from Redstone, where he read books. It came into his mind that he would tell the noble deeds of the English.

A General note on La3amon's *Brut*

La3amon's *Brut* is an early Middle English text that survives in two manuscript copies. It was composed sometime between 1155 and 1275. The *Brut* is a translation of the Anglo-Norman poem of Wace, itself a translation of the Latin prose of Geoffrey of Monmouth. It's an interstitial text: not quite Old English, not yet the easy Middle English of Chaucer. Whether La3amon wrote poetry or alliterative prose with occasional rhyme is a matter for scholarly debate.

In modern editions, the *Brut* is printed as a poem and runs to 16,000 lines. It's known to few readers outside the shrinking circle of students of medieval literature. Even amongst those students, not many read it all the way through and I suspect very few re-read it for pleasure.

The *Brut* tells the Legendary History of Britain, from its founding by Brutus, who gives the country its name, to the reign of Athelstan. It contains amongst many other things the earliest surviving English version of the King Arthur story, as well as the story of King Lear and his daughters. It would not be too mischievous to claim that what starts for us as legend ends by moving into a form of history, but the distinction, like the distinction between poetry and prose, is ours, not his.

Though the details vary, both manuscripts of the *Brut* begin by identifying La3amon as a priest, living at the small church and settlement of Areley Kings, on the banks of the Severn, about ten miles upstream from Worcester. His name, which isn't English, means Lawman, and is often modernized as such, or as Layamon.

Who he was, beyond the little he tells us, no one knows. Why he wrote in English, when he wrote and how he wrote, who he wrote it for, are all matters for scholarly speculation and there is not enough evidence to do much more than speculate.

The Red Queen

This is not explicitly in the *Brut*. However; the 'Matter of Britain' was old when La3amon was writing. It had already exerted a gravitational pull on stories that were even older than itself. In each retelling the stories became a palimpsest, created by repetition, addition, misunderstanding and forgetting. Brutus and Locrin are legendary figures, but historical tin traders had been visiting Britain regularly since the Bronze Age. Buried in the foundations of the stories about the last Trojans finding a home in Britain may be a dim memory of those Mediterranean Bronze Age traders.

Three stories from Gerald of Wales

Gerald of Wales, or Gerald the Welshman (1145-1223), is one of the more fascinating characters of the twelfth century. A highly-educated, nobly born cleric, he made a career out of annoying people. He lectured Kings and Prelates, undeterred by the fact they weren't listening to him, and he was witty, curious and an insatiable collector of stories. His 'Journey through Wales' can be read for pleasure, partly because Gerald takes breaks from telling the reader how brilliant he is, and how wrong everyone else is, to tell stories like these.

An Preost wes on leoden

The *Brut* and its author, perhaps the first English 'poet' after the Conquest to claim a text as his own, raise numerous questions. At a time when Latin was the international language of learning and French the language of the ruling classes, why Laȝamon wrote in English remains a puzzle. What such an obviously capable man was doing at Areley is another mystery. This section plays with speculative answers.

1218.
To resort to English understatement, dating the *Brut* is problematic. It must have been started after 1155. But the date by which it has to have been completed depends on the dating of the manuscripts and this has been placed as late as the last quarter of the 13th century. I have chosen 1218 because it puts him at the end of King John's reign. It is difficult not to read the poem as a reflection and commentary on kingship. The Kings of 'England' from William I to Henry III would be at home in the *Brut*. While Henry II at the height of his power would rank with the greatest of the *Brut's* Kings, John would epitomize everything that makes a King bad in the poem.

To Ireland…
J.S.P. Tatlock thought Laȝamon had been in Ireland, but there is no real evidence to place him there, or in the household of Gerald of Wales. The details of the Irish expedition made in 1185 by John, with Gerald as his 'tutor', are historical including the beard pulling. Gerald's dislike of the Irish is one reading of his writing on Ireland. Gerald quotes Pliny in his autobiographical writings, to console himself when he withdrew from the court.

First Lackland, soon Softsword…
Unflattering contemporary nicknames for John. His marriage to Isabella of Angoulême was a politically ill-judged move. It was obvious it would have bad consequences, but he went ahead and married her.

Have you heard what happened to whatsisname?
His name was William de Briouze. He had been close to Richard I and a staunch supporter of John in his early years. But he later fell out with

John and fled his justice. His wife and son were imprisoned and starved to death. Their bodies were discovered as described.

Could never keep her mouth shut.
One of the scandals of John's reign was the murder of his nephew, Arthur. Arthur was in de Briouze's custody at the time and whether he did it, or John did, or they both organized someone else to do it, Arthur was dead and the idea of being a hostage in King John's hands became unattractive. Five years later, in 1208, when John sent for the de Briouze children, Matilda was reported to have said: 'I will not deliver up my sons to your Lord, King John, because he basely murdered his nephew, Arthur, who he ought to have kept in honourable custody'. William was reportedly shocked by his wife's outspokenness. The comment may explain why John's later treatment of Matilda was so vindictive.

During the Interdict
Pope Innocent III placed John's kingdom under Interdict, which lasted from 1208 until mid 1214. During that time churches were locked and the sacraments, other than baptism and the confession of the dying, were forbidden. The actual details of what was and wasn't allowed seemed to vary but what a Parish priest did for these five years is hard to fathom. If you wanted to find a time when a Parish priest could travel looking for books, or write 16,000 lines of verse, then this five-year period is as good as any.

I don't see any reason to doubt Laȝamon's claim that he travelled looking for books.

Wasn't her beauty also *weorc wuldorfæder*?
Gerald would have answered with a resounding NO! Throughout the latter half of the 12th century the church's push towards clerical celibacy was growing stronger as was the rancid strain of misogyny that characterizes so much clerical writing in the period and is so prevalent in some of Gerald's.

At Lincoln…
Forces loyal to the child King, Henry III, led by an aging William Marshall, won an improbable victory at Lincoln in 1217 against the French and restored the shaky Angevin rule.

Fathers

The story of Gwendolin, Locrin and Aestrild follows the narrative arc of Laȝamon's version in outline. Following Laȝamon's own practice, I have expanded the story in places.

Why Locrin hides her in 'an earth house', with 'whalebone doors', is a mystery but I think the symbolism might once have been meaningful, even if it was no longer clear what that meaning was when Laȝamon was writing.

Although Laȝamon is writing after the early 'Romances' of Chrétien de Troyes, in his work love is not magnificent or tragic, but destructive. In the *Brut* lovers are not the tragic heroes they become in later medieval literature. A King who puts personal desire before duty inevitably brings trouble to the people. This is part of a larger pattern in the poem where the obligations that come with the social role always take precedent over any personal ambitions or desires.

Two stories from Bede

Oswald, King of Northumbria was defeated by Penda of Mercia in 642. Oswald's body was dismembered and his head and limbs displayed on stakes. A year later, Oswald's brother and successor, Oswiu, lead what modern media would describe as a 'daring raid deep behind enemy lines' to recover his brother's head, hand and arm.

The story about the raven is told by Reginald of Durham in the twelfth century. Oswald went on to be a celebrated saint; Oswiu to defeat Penda (655) and become possibly the only King of 'Northumbria' in the seventh century to die in his bed of what we might call natural causes.

The details of Sigbert's story are basically as told by Bede. He was another of Penda's victims.

Fragments

The End of Roman Britain is another of the great puzzles of history. Whether it fell, was pushed, decayed, or simply morphed remains obscure.

La3amon knew a version of the traditional invasion narrative, enshrined in the *Anglo-Saxon Chronicle* and the writings of Bede, in which Germanic mercenaries lead by Hengist and Horsa were originally hired to protect the Britons and then overran the country, exterminating the Britons and forcing the few survivors into the harder rocky corners of the Island.

Today this narrative no longer seems tenable. Whatever happened between the end of the fourth century and the end of the sixth, and the change was from a Roman Province to the beginnings of a recognisably 'English' country split into tribal kingdoms, varied considerably from place to place. *Fragments* picks this up. There is no overarching narrative. The fragments end by pointing forward towards the next story of Vortigern, Hengist and Rowena. Vortigern is one of the few characters in the *Brut* whom La3amon vilifies. Authorial comments are rare, often enigmatic, but the audience is left in no doubt about his contempt for Vortigern.

Bagaudae…
I have probably misused this term to denote rebellious slaves. The term is used to describe roving, lawless groups on the continent in the third and then the fifth century. Exactly what the term meant and who it was applied to seems uncertain.

However, there is no evidence for their existence in Britain but the term is too useful not to use here.

Old Scores…
Brigantes, Atrebates, Cats were British tribes, the latter being a shortened from of Catuvelluani. It has been argued that the pre-Roman tribal groups reasserted themselves in the early fifth century

West Stow…
There's an experimental archaeological site there now, open to the public and worth a visit, but about 410 it was settled by Germanic incomers. The site was not fortified. One of the problems for historians and archeologists of the period is distinguishing between a Germanic incomer and a non-Germanic resident, especially if they were peacefully sharing the same site.

Foederati…

essentially barbarian warriors who fought for Rome under special arrangements. The traditional narrative of the Anglo-Saxon arrival is that they arrived first as Foederati and then took over.

Presentment of Englishry

The question the speaker is not answering is: Are you English? A *Presentment of Englishry* in the 11th century was the offering of proof that a slain person was English (therefore unimportant), in order to escape the fine levied upon hundred or township for the murder of a 'Frenchman' or 'Norman'.

Gehyrest þu?: do you hear and understand and/or are you listening?

Lightning Source UK Ltd.
Milton Keynes UK
UKHW011816250219
337746UK00001B/10/P

9 781848 616622